OPINION

ON THE

CONSTITUTIONAL POWER OF THE MILITARY

TO

TRY AND EXECUTE

THE

ASSASSINS OF THE PRESIDENT.

By ATTORNEY GENERAL JAMES SPEED.

WASHINGTON:
GOVERNMENT PRINTING OFFICE.
1865.

OPINION

ON THE

CONSTITUTIONAL POWER OF THE MILITARY

TO

TRY AND EXECUTE

THE

ASSASSINS OF THE PRESIDENT.

BY ATTORNEY GENERAL JAMES SPEED.

WASHINGTON:
GOVERNMENT PRINTING OFFICE.
1865.

OPINION.

ATTORNEY GENERAL'S OFFICE,
Washington, July —, 1865.

SIR: You ask me whether the persons charged with the offence of having assassinated the President can be tried before a military tribunal, or must they be tried before a civil court.

The President was assassinated at a theatre in the city of Washington. At the time of the assassination a civil war was flagrant, the city of Washington was defended by fortifications regularly and constantly manned, the principal police of the city was by federal soldiers, the public offices and property in the city were all guarded by soldiers, and the President's House and person were or should have been under the guard of soldiers. Martial law had been declared in the District of Columbia, but the civil courts were open and held their regular sessions, and transacted business as in times of peace.

Such being the facts, the question is one of great importance—important, because it involves the constitutional guarantees thrown about the rights of the citizen, and because the security of the army and the government in time of war is involved; important, as it involves a seeming conflict betwixt the laws of peace and of war.

Having given the question propounded the patient and earnest consideration its magnitude and importance require, I will proceed to give the reasons why I am of the opinion that the conspirators not only may but ought to be tried by a military tribunal.

A civil court of the United States is created by a law of Congress under and according to the Constitution. To the Constitution and the law we must look to ascertain how the court is constituted, the limits of its jurisdiction, and what its mode of procedure.

A military tribunal exists under and according to the Constitution in time of war. Congress may prescribe how all such tribunals are to be constituted, what shall be their jurisdiction and mode of procedure. Should Congress fail to create such tribunals, then, under the Constitution, they must be constituted according to the laws and usages of civilized warfare. They may take cognizance of such offences as the laws of war permit; they must proceed according to the customary usages of such tribunals in time of war, and inflict such punishments as are sanctioned by the practice of civilized nations in time of war. In time of peace neither Congress nor the military can create any military tribunals, except such as are made in pursuance of that clause of the Constitution which gives to Congress the power "to make rules for the government of the land and naval forces." I do not think that Congress can, in time of war or peace, under this clause of the Constitution, create military tribunals for the adjudication of offences committed by persons not engaged in, or belonging to, such forces. This is a proposition too plain for argument. But it does not follow that because such military tribunals cannot be created by Congress under this clause, that they cannot be created at all. Is there no other power conferred by the Constitution upon Congress or the military under which such tribunals may be created in time of war?

That the law of nations constitutes a part of the laws of the land, must be admitted. The laws of nations are expressly made laws of the land by the Constitution, when it says that "Congress shall have power to define and punish piracies and felonies committed on the high seas and offences against the laws of nations." To *define* is to give the limits or precise meaning of a word or thing in being; to make, is to call into being. Congress has power to *define*, not to make, the laws of nations; but Congress has the power to make rules for the government of the army and navy. From the very face of the Constitution, then, it is evident that the laws of nations do constitute a part of the laws of the land. But very soon after the organization of the federal government, Mr. Randolph, then Attorney General, said: "The law of nations, although not specifically adopted by the Constitution, is essentially a part of the law of the land. Its obligation commences and runs with the existence of a nation, subject to modification on some points of indifference." (See opinion Attorney General, vol. 1, page 27.) The framers of the Constitution knew that a nation could not maintain an honorable place amongst the nations of the world that does not regard the great and essential principles of the law of nations as a part of the law of the land. Hence Congress may define those laws, but cannot abrogate them, or, as Mr. Randolph says, may "modify on some points of indifference."

That the laws of nations constitute a part of the laws of the land is established from the face of the Constitution, upon principle and by authority.

But the laws of war constitute much the greater part of the law of nations. Like the other laws of nations, they exist and are of binding force upon the departments and citizens of the government, though not defined by any law of Congress. No one that has ever glanced at the many treatises that have been published in different ages of the world by great, good, and learned men, can fail to know that the laws of war constitute a part of the law of nations, and that those laws have been prescribed with tolerable accuracy.

Congress can declare war. When war is declared, it must be, under the Constitution, carried on according to the known laws and usages of war amongst civilized nations. Under the power to define those laws,

Congress cannot abrogate them or authorize their infraction. The Constitution does not permit this government to prosecute a war as an uncivilized and barbarous people.

As war is required by the frame-work of our government to be prosecuted according to the known usages of war amongst the civilized nations of the earth, it is important to understand what are the obligations, duties, and responsibilities imposed by war upon the military. Congress, not having defined, as under the Constitution it might have done, the laws of war, we must look to the usage of nations to ascertain the powers conferred in war, on whom the exercise of such powers devolve, over whom, and to what extent do those powers reach, and in how far the citizen and the soldier are bound by the legitimate use thereof.

The power conferred by war is, of course, adequate to the end to be accomplished, and not greater than what is necessary to be accomplished. The law of war, like every other code of laws, declares what shall not be done, and does not say what may be done. The legitimate use of the great power of war, or rather the prohibitions upon the use of that power, increase or diminish as the necessity of the case demands. When a city is besieged and hard pressed, the commander may exert an authority over the non-combatants which he may not when no enemy is near.

All wars against a domestic enemy or to repel invasions are prosecuted to preserve the government. If the invading force can be overcome by the ordinary civil police of a country, it should be done without bringing upon the country the terrible scourge of war; if a commotion or insurrection can be put down by the ordinary process of law, the military should not be called out. A defensive foreign war is declared and carried on because the civil police is inadequate to repel it; a civil war is waged because the laws cannot be peacefully enforced by the ordinary tribunals of the country through civil process and by civil officers. Because of the utter inability to keep the peace and maintain order by the customary officers and agencies in time of peace, armies are organized and put into the field. They are called out and invested with the powers of war to prevent total anarchy and to preserve the government. Peace is the normal condition of a country, and war abnormal, neither being without law, but each having laws appropriate to the condition of society. The maxim *inter arma silent leges* is never wholly true. The object of war is to bring society out of its abnormal condition; and the laws of war aim to have that done with the least possible injury to persons or property.

Anciently, when two nations were at war, the conqueror had or asserted the right to take from his enemy his life, liberty, and property: if either was spared, it was as a favor or act of mercy. By the laws of nations, and of war as a part thereof, the conqueror was deprived of this right.

When two governments, foreign to each other, are at war, or when a civil war becomes territorial, all of the people of the respective belligerents become by the law of nations the enemies of each other. As enemies they cannot hold intercourse, but neither can kill or injure the other except under a commission from their respective governments. So humanizing have been and are the laws of war, that it is a high offence against them to kill an enemy without such commission. The laws of war demand that a man shall not take human life except under a license from his government; and under the Constitution of the United States no license can be given by any department of the government to take human life in war, except according to the law and usages of war. Soldiers regularly in the service have the license of the government to deprive men, the active enemies of their government, of their liberty and lives; their commission so to act is as perfect and legal as that of a judge to adjudicate, but the soldier must act in obedience to the laws of war, as the judge must in obedience to the civil law. A civil judge must try criminals in the mode prescribed in the Constitution and the law; so, soldiers must kill or capture according to the laws of war. Non-combatants are not to be disturbed or interfered with by the armies of either party except in extreme cases. Armies are called out and organized to meet and overcome the active, acting public enemies.

But enemies with which an army has to deal are of two classes:

1st. Open, active participants in hostilities, as soldiers who wear the uniform, move under the flag, and hold the appropriate commission from their government. Openly assuming to discharge the duties and meet the responsibilities and dangers of soldiers, they are entitled to all belligerent rights, and should receive all the courtesies due to soldiers. The true soldier is proud to acknowledge and respect those rights, and ever cheerfully extends those courtesies.

2d. Secret, but active participants, as spies, brigands, bushwhackers, jayhawkers, war rebels, and assassins. In all wars, and especially in civil wars, such secret, active enemies rise up to annoy and attack an army, and they must be met and put down by the army. When lawless wretches become so impudent and powerful as not to be controlled and governed by the ordinary tribunals of a country, armies are called out, and the laws of war invoked. Wars never have been and never can be conducted upon the principle that an army is but a *posse comitatis* of a civil magistrate.

An army, like all other organized bodies, has a right, and it is its first duty, to protect its own existence, and the existence of all its parts, by the means and in the mode usual among civilized nations when at war. Then the question arises, do the laws of war authorize a different mode of proceeding and the use of different means against secret active enemies from those used against open active enemies?

As has been said, the open enemy or soldier in time of war may be met in battle and killed, wounded, or taken prisoner, or so placed by the lawful strategy of war as that he is powerless. Unless the law of self-preservation absolutely demands it, the life of a wounded enemy or a prisoner must be spared. Unless pressed thereto by the extremest necessity, the laws of war condemn and punish with great severity harsh or cruel treatment to a wounded enemy or a prisoner.

Certain stipulations and agreements, tacit or express, betwixt the open belligerent parties, are permitted by the laws of war, and are held to be of very high and sacred character. Such is the tacit understanding, or it may be usage, of war, in regard to flags of truce. Flags of truce are resorted to as a means of saving human life, or alleviating human suffering. When not used with perfidy, the laws of war require that they should be respected. The Romans regarded ambassadors betwixt belligerents as persons to be treated with consideration and respect. Plutarch, in his Life of Cæsar, tells us that the barbarians in Gaul having sent some ambassadors to Cæsar, he detained them, charging fraudulent practices, and led his army to battle, obtaining a great victory.

When the senate decreed festivals and sacrifices for the victory, Cato declared it to be his opinion that Cæsar ought to be given into the hands of the barbarians, that so the guilt which this breach of faith might otherwise bring upon the state might be expiated by transferring the curse on him who was the occasion of it.

Under the Constitution and laws of the United States, should a commander be guilty of such a flagrant breach of law as Cato charged upon Cæsar, he would not be delivered to the enemy, but would be punished after a military trial. The many honorable gentlemen who hold commissions in the army of the United States, and have been deputed to conduct war according to the laws of war, would keenly feel it as an insult to their profession of arms for any one to say that they could not or would not punish a fellow-soldier who was guilty of wanton cruelty to a prisoner, or perfidy towards the bearers of a flag of truce.

The laws of war permit capitulations of surrender and paroles. They are agreements betwixt belligerents, and should be scrupulously observed and performed. They are contracts wholly unknown to civil tribunals. Parties to such contracts must answer any breaches thereof to the customary military tribunals in time of war. If an officer of rank, possessing the pride that becomes a soldier and a gentleman, who should capitulate to surrender the forces and property under his command and control, be charged with a fraudulent breach of the terms of surrender, the laws of war do not permit that he should be punished without a trial, or, if innocent, that he shall have no means of wiping out the foul imputation. If a paroled prisoner is charged with a breach of his parole, he may be punished if guilty, but not without a trial. He should be tried by a military tribunal constituted and proceeding as the laws and usages of war prescribe.

The law and usage of war contemplate that soldiers have a high sense of personal honor. The true soldier is proud to feel and to know that his enemy possesses personal honor, and will conform and be obedient to the laws of war. In a spirit of justice, and with a wise appreciation of such feelings, the laws of war protect the character and honor of an open enemy. When by the fortunes of war one open enemy is thrown into the hands and power of another, and is charged with dishonorable conduct and a breach of the laws of war, he must be tried according to the usages of war. Justice and fairness say that an open enemy to whom dishonorable conduct is imputed, has a right to demand a trial. If such a demand can be rightfully made, surely it cannot be rightfully refused. It is to be hoped that the military authorities of this country will never refuse such a demand, because there is no act of Congress that authorizes it. In time of war the law and usage of war authorize it, and they are a part of the law of the land.

One belligerent may request the other to punish for breaches of the laws of war, and, regularly, such a request should be made before retaliatory measures are taken. Whether the laws of war have been infringed or not, is of necessity a question to be decided by the laws and usages of war, and is cognizable before a military tribunal. When prisoners of war conspire to escape or are guilty of a breach of appropriate and necessary rules of prison discipline, they may be punished, but not without trial. The commander who should order every prisoner charged with improper conduct to be shot or hung, would be guilty of a high offence against the laws of war, and should be punished therefor, after a regular military trial. If the culprit should be condemned and executed, the commander would be as free from guilt as if the man had been killed in battle.

It is manifest, from what has been said, that military tribunals exist under and according to the laws and usages of war in the interest of justice and mercy. They are established to save human life, and to prevent cruelty as far as possible. The commander of an army in time of war has the same power to organize military tribunals and execute their judgments that he has to set his squadrons in the field and fight battles. His authority in each case is from the law and usage of war.

Having seen that there must be military tribunals to decide questions arising in time of war betwixt belligerents who are open and active enemies, let us next see whether the laws of war do not authorize such tribunals to determine the fate of those who are active, but secret, participants in the hostilities.

In Mr. Wheaton's Elements of International Law, he says, "the effect of a state of war, lawfully declared to exist, is to place all the subjects of each belligerent power in a state of mutual hostility. The usage of nations has modified this maxim by legalizing such acts of hostility only as are committed by those who are authorized by the express or implied command of the state; such are the regularly commissioned naval and military forces of the nation and all others called out in its defence, or spontaneously defending themselves, in case of necessity, without any express authority for that purpose. Cicero tells us in his offices, that by the Roman feudal law no person could lawfully engage in battle with the public enemy without being regularly enrolled, and taking the military oath. This was a regulation sanctioned both by policy and religion. The horrors of war would indeed be greatly aggravated, if every individual of the belligerent states were allowed to plunder and slay indiscriminately the enemy's subjects without being in any manner accountable for his conduct. *Hence it is that, in land wars, irregular bands of marauders are liable to be treated as lawless banditti, not entitled to the protection of the mitigated usages of war as practiced by civilized nations.*" (Wheaton's Elements of International Law, page 406, 3d edition.)

In speaking upon the subject of banditti, Patrick Henry said, in the Virginia convention, "the honorable gentleman has given you an elaborate account of what he judges tyannical legislation, and an *ex post facto* law—(in the case of Josiah Phillips;) he has misrepresented the facts. That man was not executed by a tyrannical stroke of power; nor was he a Socrates; he was a fugitive murderer, and an outlaw; a man who commanded an *infamous banditti*, and *at a time when the war was at the most perilous stage* he committed the most cruel and shocking barbarities; he was an enemy to the human name. Those who declare war against the human race may be struck out of existence as soon as apprehended. He was not executed according to those beautiful legal ceremonies which are pointed out by the laws in criminal cases. The enormity of his crimes did not entitle him to it. I am truly a friend to legal forms and methods, but, sir, the occasion warranted the measure. A pirate, an outlaw, or a common enemy to all mankind, may be put to death at any time. It is jusfied by the *law of nature and nations.*" (3d volume Elliott's Debates on Federal Constitution, page 140.)

No reader, not to say student, of the law of nations, can doubt but that Mr. Wheaton and Mr. Henry have fairly stated the laws of war. Let it be constantly borne in mind that they are talking of the law in a state of war. These banditti that spring up in time of war are respecters of no law, human or divine, of peace or of war, are *hostes humani generis*, and may be hunted down like wolves. Thoroughly desperate and perfectly lawless, no man can be required to peril his life in venturing to take them prisoners—as prisoners, no trust can be reposed in them. But they are occasionally made prisoners. Being prisoners, what is to be done with them? If they are public enemies, assuming and exercising the right to kill, and are not regularly authorized to do so, they must be apprehended and dealt with by the military. No man can doubt the right and duty of the military to make prisoners of them, and being public enemies, it is the duty of the military to punish them for any infraction of the laws of war. But the military cannot ascertain whether they are guilty or not without the aid of a military tribunal.

In all wars, and especially in civil wars, secret but active enemies are almost as numerous as open ones. That fact has contributed to make civil wars such scourges to the countries in which they rage. In nearly all foreign wars the contending parties speak different languages, and have different habits and manners; but in most civil wars that is not the case; hence there is a security in participating secretly in hostilities that induces many to thus engage. War prosecuted according to the most civilized usage is horrible, but its horrors are greatly aggravated by the immemorial habits of plunder, rape, and murder practiced by secret, but active participants. Certain laws and usages have been adopted by the civilized world in wars between nations that are not of kin to one another, for the purpose and to the effect of arresting or softening many of the necessary cruel consequences of war. How strongly bound are we, then, in the midst of a great war, where brother and personal friend are fighting against brother and friend, to adopt and be governed by those laws and usages.

A public enemy must or should be dealt with in all wars by the same laws. The fact that they are public enemies, being the same, they should deal with each other according to those laws of war that are contemplated by the Constitution. Whatever rules have been adopted and practiced by the civilized nations of the world in war to soften its harshness and severity, should be adopted and practiced by us in this war. That the laws of war authorized commanders to create and establish military commissions, courts, or tribunals, for the trial of offenders against the laws of war, whether they be active or secret participants in the hostilities, cannot be denied. That the judgments of such tribunals may have been sometimes harsh, and sometimes even tyrannical, does not prove that they ought not to exist, nor does it prove that they are not constituted in the interest of justice and mercy. Considering the power that the laws of war give over secret participants in hostilities, such as banditti, guerillas, spies, &c., the position of a commander would be miserable indeed if he could not call to his aid the judgments of such tribunals; he would become a mere butcher of men, without the power to ascertain justice, and there can be no mercy where there is no justice. War in its mildest form is horrible; but take away from the contending armies the ability and right to organize what is now known as a Bureau of Military Justice, they would soon become monster savages, unrestrained by any and all ideas of law and justice. Surely no lover of mankind, no one that respects law and order, no one that has the instinct of justice, or that can be sof tened by mercy, would, in time of war, take away from the commanders the right to organize military tribunals of justice, and especially such tribunals for the protection of persons charged or suspected with being secret foes and participants in the hostilities. It would be a miracle if the records and history of this war do not show occasional cases in which those tribunals have erred; but they will show many, very many cases in which human life would have been taken but for the interposition and judgments of those tribunals. Every student of the laws of war must acknowledge that such tribunals exert a kindly and benign influence in time of war. Impartial history will record the fact that the Bureau of Military Justice, regularly organized during this war, has saved human life and prevented human suffering. The greatest suffering, patiently endured by our soldiers, and the hardest battles gallantly fought during this protracted struggle, are not more creditable to the American character than the establishment of this bureau. This people have such an educated and profound respect for law and justice—such a love of mercy—that they have, in the midst of this greatest of civil wars, systematized and brought into regular order tribunals that before this war existed under the law of war, but without general rule. To condemn the tribunals that have been established under this bureau is to condemn and denounce the war itself, or, justifying the war, to insist that it shall be prosecuted according to the harshest rules, and without the aid of the laws, usages, and customary agencies for mitigating those rules. If such tribunals had not existed before, under the laws and usages of war, the American citizen might as proudly point to their establishment as to our inimitable and inestimable constitutions. It must be constantly borne in mind that such tribunals and such a bureau cannot exist except in time of war, and cannot then take cognizance of offenders or offences where the civil courts are open, except offenders and offences against the laws of war.

But it is insisted by some, and doubtless with honesty, and with a zeal commensurate with their honesty, that such military tribunals can have no constitutional existence. The argument against their constitutionality may be shortly, and I think fairly, stated thus:

Congress alone can establish military or civil judicial tribunals. As Congress has not established military tribunals, except such as have been created under the articles of war, and which articles are made in pursuance of that clause in the Constitution which gives to Congress the power to make rules for the government of the army and navy, any other tribunal is and must be plainly unconstitutional, and all its acts void.

This objection thus stated, or stated in any other way, begs the question. It assumes that Congress alone can establish military judicial tribunals. Is that assumption true?

We have seen that when war comes, the laws and usages of war come also, and that during the war they are a part of the laws of the land. Under the Constitution, Congress may define and punish offences against those laws, but in default of Congress's defining those laws and prescribing a punishment for their infraction, and the mode of proceeding to ascertain whether an offence has been committed, and what punishment is to be inflicted, the army must be governed by the laws and usages of war as understood and practiced by the civilized nations of the world It has been abundantly shown that these tribunals are constituted by the army in the interest of justice and mercy, and for the purpose and to the effect of mitigating the horrors of war.

But it may be insisted that though the laws of war, being a part of the law of nations, constitute a part of the laws of the land, that those laws must be regarded as modified so far and whenever they come in direct conflict with plain constitutional provisions. The following clauses of the Constitution are principally relied upon to show the conflict betwixt the laws of war and the Constitution:

"The trial of all crimes, except in cases of impeachment, shall be by the jury; and such trial shall be held in the State where the said crime shall have been committed; but when not committed within any State, the trial shall be at such place or places as the Congress may by law have directed." (Art. III of the original Constitution, sec. 2.)

"No person shall be held to answer for a capital or otherwise infamous crime unless on a presentment or indictment of a grand jury, except in cases arising in the land or naval forces, or in the militia when in actual service, in time of war or public danger; nor shall any person be subject for the same offence to be twice put in jeopardy of life or limb, nor shall be compelled, in any criminal case, to be witness against himself, nor be deprived of life, liberty, or property, without due process of law; nor shall private property be taken for public use without just compensation."—(Amendments to the Constitution, Art. V.)

"In all criminal prosecutions, the accused shall enjoy the right to a speedy and public trial by an impartial jury of the State and district wherein the crime shall have been committed, which district shall have been previously ascertained by law, and be informed of the nature and cause of the accusation; to be confronted with the witnesses against him, to have compulsory process for obtaining witnesses in his favor; and to have the assistance of counsel for his defence."—(Art. VI of the amendments to the Constitution.)

These provisions of the Constitution are intended to fling around the life, liberty, and property of a citizen all the guarantees of a jury trial. These constitutional guarantees cannot be estimated too highly, or protected too sacredly. The reader of history knows that for many weary ages the people suffered for the want of them; it would not only be stupidity, but madness in us not to preserve them. No man has a deeper conviction of their value or a more sincere desire to preserve and perpetuate them than I have.

Nevertheless, these exalted and sacred provisions of the Constitution must not be read alone and by themselves, but must be read and taken in connexion with other provisions. The Constitution was framed by great men, men of learning and large experience, and it is a wonderful monument of their wisdom. Well versed in the history of the world, they knew that the nation for which they were forming a government would, unless all history was false, have wars, foreign and domestic. Hence the government framed by them is clothed with the power to make and carry on war. As has been shown, when war comes, the laws of war come with it. Infractions of the laws of nations are not denominated *crimes*, but *offences*. Hence the expression in the Constitution that "Congress shall have power to define and punish * * *offences* against the law of nations." Many of the *offences* against the law of nations for which a man may, by the laws of war, lose his life, his liberty, or his property, are not *crimes*. It is an offence against the law of nations to break a lawful blockade, and for which a forfeiture of the property is the penalty, and yet the running a blockade has never been regarded a crime; to hold communication or intercourse with the enemy is a high offence against the laws of war, and for which those laws prescribe punishment, and yet it is not a *crime;* to act as spy is an offence against the laws of war, and the punishment for which in all ages has been death, and yet it is not a crime; to violate a flag of truce is an offence against the laws of war, and yet not a crime of which a civil court can take cognizance; to unite with banditti, jayhawkers, guerillas, or any other unauthorized marauders is a high offence against the laws of war; the offence is complete when the band is organized or joined. The atrocities committed by such a band do not constitute the offence, but make the reasons, and sufficient reasons they are, why such banditti are denounced by the laws of war. Some of the offences against the laws of war are crimes, and some not. Because they are crimes they do not cease to be offences against those laws; nor because they are not crimes or misdemeanors do they fail to be offences against the laws of war. Murder is a crime, and the murderer as such must be proceeded against in the form and manner prescribed in the Constitution; in committing the murder an offence may also have been committed against the laws of war; for that offence he must answer to the laws of war, and the tribunals legalized by that law.

There is, then, an apparent but no real conflict in the constitutional provisions. *Offences* against the laws of war must be dealt with and punished under the Constitution as the laws of war, they being a part of the law of nations direct; *crimes* must be dealt with and punished as the Constitution, and laws made in pursuance thereof, may direct.

Congress has not undertaken to define the code of war nor to punish offences against it. In the case of a spy, Congress has undertaken to say who shall be deemed a spy, and how he shall be punished. But every lawyer knows that a spy was a well known offender under the laws of war, and that under and according to those laws he could have been tried and punished without an act of Congress. This is admitted by the act of Congress, when it says that he shall suffer death "according to the law and usages of war." The act is simply declaratory of the law.

That portion of the Constitution which declares that "no person shall be deprived of his life, liberty, or property without due process of law," has such direct reference to, and connexion with, trials for *crime* or *criminal* prosecutions that comment upon it would seem to be unnecessary. Trials for offences against the laws of war are not embraced or intended to be embraced in those provisions. If this is not so, then every man that kills another in battle is a murderer, for he deprived a "person of life without that due process of law" contemplated by this provision; every man who holds another as a prisoner of war is liable for false imprisonment, as he does so without that due process of law contemplated by this provision; every soldier that marches across a field in battle array is liable to an action of trespass, because he does it without that same due process. The argument that flings around offenders against the laws of war these guarantees of the Constitution would convict all the soldiers of our army of murder; no prisoners could be taken and held; the army could not move. The absurd consequences that would of necessity flow from such an argument show that it cannot be the true construction—it cannot be what was intended by the framers of the instrument. One of the prime motives for the Union and a federal government was to confer the powers of war. If any provisions of the Constitution are so in conflict with the power to carry on war as to destroy and make it valueless, then the instrument, instead of being a great and wise one, is a miserable failure, a *felo de se*.

If a man should sue out his writ of *habeas corpus*, and the return shows that he belonged to the army or navy, and was held to be tried for some offence against the rules and articles of war, the writ should be dismissed and the party remanded to answer to the charges. So, in time of war, if a man should sue out a writ of *habeas corpus*, and it is made appear that he is in the hands of the military as a prisoner of war, the writ should be dismissed and the prisoner remanded to be disposed of as the laws and usages of war require. If the prisoner be a regular unoffending soldier of the opposing party to the war, he should be treated with all the courtesy and kindness consistent with his safe custody; if he has offended against the laws of war, he should have such trial and be punished as the laws of war require. A spy, though a prisoner of war, may be tried, condemned, and executed by a military tribunal without a breach of the Constitution. A bushwhacker, a jayhawker, a bandit, a war rebel, an assassin, being public enemies, may be tried, condemned, and executed as offenders against the laws of war. The soldier that would fail to try a spy or bandit after his capture would be as derelict in duty as if he were to fail to capture; he is as much bound to try and to execute, if guilty, as he is to arrest; the same law that makes it his duty to pursue and kill or capture makes it his duty to try according to the usages of war. The judge of a civil court is not more strongly bound under the Constitution and the law to try a criminal than is the military to try an offender against the laws of war.

The fact that the civil courts are open does not affect the right of the military tribunal to hold as a prisoner and to try. The civil courts have no more right to prevent the military, in time of war, from trying an offender against the laws of war than they have a right to interfere with and prevent a battle. A battle may be lawfully fought in the very view and presence of a court; so a spy, a bandit, or other offender against the law of war may be tried, and tried lawfully, when and where the civil courts are open and transacting the usual business.

The laws of war authorize human life to be taken without legal process, or that legal process contemplated by those provisions in the Constitution that are relied upon to show that military judicial tribunals are unconstitutional. Wars should be prosecuted justly as well as bravely. One enemy in the power of another, whether he be an open or a secret one, should not be punished or executed without trial. If the question be one concerning the laws of war, he should be tried by those engaged in the war—they and they only are his peers. The military must decide whether he is or not an active participant in the hostilities. If he is an active participant in the hostilities, it is the duty of the military to take him a prisoner without warrant or other judicial process, and dispose of him as the laws of war direct.

It is curious to see one and the same mind justify the killing of thousands in battle because it is done according to the laws of war, and yet condemning that same law when, out of regard for justice and with the hope of saving life, it orders a military trial before the enemy are killed. The love of law, of justice, and the wish to save life and suffering, should impel all good men in time of war to uphold and sustain the existence and action of such tribunals. The object of such tribunals is obviously intended to save life, and when their jurisdiction is confined to offences against the laws of war, that is their effect. They prevent indiscriminate slaughter; they prevent men from being punished or killed upon mere suspicion.

The law of nations, which is the result of the experience and wisdom of ages, has decided that jayhawkers, banditti, &c., are offenders against the laws of nature, and of war, and as such amenable to the military. Our Constitution has made those laws a part of the law of the land. Obedience to the Constitution and the law, then, requires that the military should do their whole duty; they must not only meet and fight the enemies of the country in open battle, but they must kill or take the secret enemies of the country, and try and execute them according to the laws of war. The civil tribunals of the country cannot rightfully interfere with the military in the performance of their high, arduous, and perilous, but lawful duties. That Booth and his associates were secret active public enemies, no mind that contemplates the facts can doubt. The exclamation used by him when he escaped from the box on to the stage, after he had fired the fatal shot, *sic semper tyrannis*, and his dying message, "say to my mother that I died for my country," show that he was not an assassin from private malice, but that he acted as a public foe. Such a deed is expressly laid down by Vattel, in his work on the law of nations, as an offence against the laws of war, and a great crime. "I give, then, the name of assassination to a treacherous murder, whether the perpetrators of the deed be the subjects of the party whom we cause to be assassinated or of our own sovereign, or that it be executed by any other emissary introducing himself as a suppliant, a refugee, or a deserter, or, in fine, as a stranger." (Vattel, 339.)

Neither the civil nor the military department of the government should regard itself as wiser and better than the Constitution and the laws that exist under or are made in pursuance thereof. Each department should, in peace and in war, confining itself to its own proper sphere of action, diligently and fearlessly perform its legitimate functions, and in the mode prescribed by the Constitution and the law. Such obedience to and observance of law will maintain peace when it exists, and will soonest relieve the country from the abnormal state of war.

My conclusion, therefore, is, that if the persons who are charged with the assassination of the President committed the deed as public enemies, as I believe they did, and whether they did or not is a question to be decided by the tribunal before which they are tried, they not only can, but ought to be tried before a military tribunal. If the persons charged have offended against the laws of war, it would be as palpably wrong for the military to hand them over to the civil courts, as it would be wrong in a civil court to convict a man of murder who had, in time of war, killed another in battle.

I am, sir, most respectfully, your obedient servant,

JAMES SPEED, *Attorney General.*

To the PRESIDENT.

www.ingramcontent.com/pod-product-compliance
Lightning Source LLC
La Vergne TN
LVHW020637110826
845149LV00004B/1246
* 9 7 8 1 4 1 8 1 9 0 7 3 6 *